OVERCOMING
ADVERSITY

OVERCOMING ADVERSITY:
HANDLING ANY SITUATION WITH GODLY STRENGTH

DR. CARL GARRIGUS

CROSSLINK PUBLISHING

CrossLink Publishing
www.crosslinkpublishing.com

ISBN 978-1-63357-086-3
Library of Congress Control Number: 2016952379

CONTENTS

THE OPPORTUNITY LIFE

James 1:1-4 - Use life's circumstances to develop perfect faith

The cancer had taken its toll and I could fake bravery no longer. There I was curled up in a ball crying my eyes out. It had been two hours and I was officially broken. Finishing another day of working on my will in preparation for possibly dying, while in the morning putting together my soon-to-be-born daughter's crib had become too much. As I lay on the floor at the end of my rope, talking to God, this wave of understanding came over me. Slowly coming to my knees, with bowed head, I truly experienced the presence of God as He spoke and gave direction. It was as if the world had stopped and only God and I existed in the universe. Wiping away the tears I said aloud in response to His whispers: "OK God, I understand." I went downstairs, opened my Bible, and read the first section of James.

The first four verses of James are the lynchpin for the entire book. Throughout the letter James gives practical advice on how to grow in faith, and his ultimate conclusion—merely professing faith isn't enough for a Christian walk to be fully committed—rests squarely on his crucial points in verses 1–4. The key takeaway: trials and difficult times are opportunities to spiritually mature. Developing perfect faith is the path to an extraordinary life of joy, peace, and contentment.

Verse 1: "To the twelve tribes which are scattered abroad:"

Verse 1 establishes a very important point related to the intended audience. It might be tempting to notice the reference to the twelve tribes. A number of Jewish references pepper the book and certainly much of it would be familiar to Jews of the time, but focusing on the twelve tribes would miss the point: the book is written to all of us. The key word is "scattered." While the book definitely predates the destruction of the Jerusalem Temple in AD 70, the Jewish diaspora had been going on for quite some time, so the Jews already had a history of being scattered. "Scattered" suggests people experiencing a loss, experiencing trouble, and we have all been there. The world is broken and trouble is behind, in front, and right around the corner. We all know that. Sometimes it feels as if I'm going from one crisis to another or merely trying to keep my head above water as multiple things crash into my life. Maybe you feel the same way. All of us know loss and trouble. James is writing to everyone; he is writing directly to your precious heart.

Verses 2–3: "My brethren, count it all joy when you fall into various trials, knowing that the testing of your faith produces patience."

When first encountering these verses, they gave me a great deal of angst. At the time I thought God was trying to say when a trial hits, the response should be a skip in my step and a smile on my face. Wrapping my brain around such a concept was incredibly difficult because it felt so unnatural and I felt quite incapable. I had it wrong.

God is not saying you need to proclaim "Yay!" when the doctor gives the bad news or when the boss calls you into the office for a "talk." God completely understands the freak out after receiving bad news; He knows a first reaction might be sadness, anger, anxiety, stress, and a whole host of other painful emotions. Notice how the verse says when you fall *into* various trials. It is not necessary to be joyous *for* the trial but develop joy *in* the trial. Don't focus on avoiding trials or fixing the problem but concentrate on allowing God to reveal its godly purpose. Obviously if your house is burning down, don't stand in the living room contemplating how much joy you have. Immediate feelings may be negative or self-centered, but as soon as possible turn to God and recognize the trial for what it really is: an opportunity. The trouble comes when, in an effort to become the master, we try to manipulate and control to create the desired outcome.

I hate to be the bearer of bad news, but working as feverishly as possible and trying to manipulate circumstances won't change the outcome because a trial is going to continue as long as the omnipotent ruler of the universe wants it to last. Now this might be difficult to feel in your heart because so much of our society is built around the idea of fleeing pain and finding pleasure. We have sold our souls to the devil as a society to try to create the illusion of living an easy life, one without burdens and worries. Foolishly, the perception has become security is a product of money and possessions and power, which is sought with reckless self-empowerment in everything from selfies and social media status to homes and cars. Messages from ads and pop culture hold out the promise of control, power, and the world at the edge of fingertips. Just grab it and possess it. Me, me, me. It's all a lie because all of those things are temporary and absolutely incapable of providing true peace, joy, and contentment. It's all a lie because the number one thing God wants you to do is live humbly, serve, and grow closer to Him. We spend so much time trying to escape trials and avoid troubles we miss the point and true depth of life, which comes from growing in faith during difficult times. God loves you and has your best interest at heart. Once a trial is seen as God sees it, the negative emotions of the freak out cease and you begin the process of working through the trial. The godly purpose of a trial is going to create a better person on the other side.

The key to getting through the trial is connected to the word "testing." Testing is a very common translation of the word from the ancient Greek texts, but we need to be clear here. Do not take the word "testing" to mean atrial is testing whether or not you have faith. This isn't a pass–fail thing. The word "testing" really means something closer to approval (Walvoord, 1983). The trial is not proving whether or not faith is present, but rather stripping away lower levels of faith to reveal, and help develop, perfect faith, which is the approved level of faith.

Rarely do people talk about it but there are degrees of faith. Perhaps the best statement on this issue is from the Lord Jesus Christ and His parable of the sower. In Matthew 13:4 Jesus talks about the seed that falls by the wayside. "And as he sowed, some seed fell by the wayside; and the birds came and devoured them." The seed is the Word of God, the birds are the forces of evil, and you are the soil. So this type of person would have the lowest level of faith, which in fact is no faith. Things happen and the person doesn't turn to God. The Word finds no soil in which to grow. Verses 5 and 6 give us the second level of faith: knowing faith. "Some fell on stony places, where they did not have much earth; and they immediately sprang up because they had no depth of earth. But when the sun was up they were scorched, and because they had no root they withered away." This is someone whose faith is very surface. It is of the head, not the heart. Tepid faith is found in verse 7: "And some fell among thorns, and thorns sprang up and choked them." As Christ clearly states in His explanation of the parable later in the chapter (verses 18–23), these are individuals who have faith but it's lukewarm, it doesn't inform their whole life and as such faith is easily tossed aside as money, power, possessions, and acceptance take precedence. In my experience there are many, many Christians who fall under this level. Then there is perfect faith, and we see this in verse 8 of the parable. This faith has deep roots and good soil, and the Word produces much fruit in these lives. No faith, knowing faith, tepid faith, and perfect faith.

These degrees of faith are only in reference to expressions of faith and should not be taken to advocate anything regarding salvation. Remember, James is not discussing salvation, so this reference to faith in verse 3 does not address a believer's legal relationship to God. Once you put faith in the Risen Lord as redeemer, your name is written in the Lamb's Book of Life and eternal salvation is secured. Rather than discussing salvation, James is writing about what happens after: the time between the moment you give your life to Christ and the moment God calls you home to Heaven. Even though the levels of faith are fluid and believers can move from one to the next, the spiritual journey is not a straight uphill climb to the top of the mountain but rather has hills and valleys. The Christian life is an expedition, not a moment. The point is to move through these times of success and failure to ever higher ground. Mistakes are inevitable but they are also awesome opportunities to learn and do better the next time. Moving to higher levels of faith comes from a concerted, deliberate effort to grow in spiritual maturity by learning from both success and failure, good times and bad.

With perfect faith an extraordinary life of peace, joy, and contentment awaits, but it doesn't come from winning the lottery or having things easy, quick, and placed on a silver platter; it only comes through the fire of trials, troubles, and difficult times. You learn more about yourself, God, and your incredible relationship with the Almighty during valleys rather than mountaintops.

I've been there many times. I've grown far closer to God going through the experience of cancer than anything else. Developing perfect faith over money came not by making a lot of it but by being fired. The purpose of trials and afflictions is to strip away all the other levels and produce a believer grounded in a state of perfect faith, the approved level. I can tell you from personal experience perfect faith—joy, peace, and contentment—is on the other side of your trial. It is through the trial perfect faith comes into an area of your life, but don't stop there.

Verse 4: "But let patience have its perfect work, that you may be perfect and complete, lacking nothing."

The Lord desires we not only take a trial and let it serve its godly purpose of developing perfect faith in one area but also to keep going through the process to develop perfect faith in all areas. This is the highest level of enlightenment one can have while here on earth. Once perfect faith is developed in all areas, life becomes completely content and this frees you to experience utter joy no matter what happens. Trading stress, anxiety, anger, and sadness for joy, peace, and contentment, to be perfect and complete and to lack nothing, sounds like a pretty good trade off to me and is something I hope everyone desires. Why settle for less when the Bible and specifically the book of James is providing a road map on how to feel perfect and complete?

I suggest you really engage in some serious emotional self-awareness and think about the areas where there exist negative emotions such as stress, anger, sadness, and anxiety. Try to be honest and think about the causes of those emotions. Now identify one of those areas. Tread carefully because the obvious choice would be the most emotionally painful one, but pray long and hard before choosing that path. A relationship with God is one that needs cultivation; it needs to develop. You have to walk before running, and God has a tendency to start people off small and to develop one area before allowing someone to take another step and embrace more responsibility. In the parable of the talents (Matthew 25:14–30), the two men who multiplied what they had been given were further blessed, but the servant who buried the money and returned just that amount had his portion taken from him. The one who had received the least amount and did nothing could not be trusted with more. When we race ahead of God, which is very common in our very impatient world, stepping outside God's will and seeking a different path leads to trouble. Think of this as a marathon, not a sprint. After identifying an important but not overly exhausting issue developing perfect faith, there should lead to more emotionally sensitive areas where the process begins again. Such a thing may seem daunting, but don't worry because help awaits, which is where the next section of the book picks up.

Five Questions for Exploration

- Is there an area of your life where you exhibit tepid or knowing faith and need to spiritually grow?
- Is there something you are going through where your immediate and prolonged reaction is negative?
- In what ways do you see a trial as an obstacle rather than an opportunity?

- Do you possess perfect faith in any area of your life? If so, how do you display your perfect faith?
- Once you develop perfect faith in one area, what is a second area of your life where you need to spiritually grow?

2

GOD THE HELPER

James 1:5–11 - We have God to help us develop perfect faith

My wife and I were going through the inevitable season in our marriage where our bond was weak: we were tired, stressed, and at each other's throats. The more I tried to get my way, the worse the situation became. Trying on our own to fix things weakened our marriage further. When we reengaged God with daily Bible study, prayer, and meditation the more clarity, patience, caring, and empathy we as a couple possessed and our marriage improved. Moving out of the way and letting God define and direct the marriage made the positive difference.

This section of the book revolves around our need for God because it is impossible to develop perfect faith on our own. Believers must take the time to seek the Lord's will, especially through prayer. Effective prayer, combined with Bible study and meditation on the Word, will enable God to reveal His will.

Verse 5: "If any of you lack wisdom, let him ask of God, who gives to all liberally and without reproach, and it will be given to him."

To develop perfect faith requires consistent, prolonged, and daily prayer, meditation, and Bible study. You simply can't get around those crucial components of the Christian walk because there are no shortcuts to a vibrant relationship with God. The number one thing the omnipotent, omniscient ruler of the universe wants is to be your best friend and such a thing takes work. To seek the Lord's will involves effort and time. We live in a world where people want fast and easy, but that is not the way of God. He wants your precious time and attention. Make spending time with God a priority, including daily prayer. Without fail, every time I get out of the habit of daily seeking the Lord in prayer and scripture life gets worse, and as soon as I reengage God through daily Bible study, prayer, and meditation, comfort and understanding how to navigate the troubled waters with confidence sink deep into my heart. This happens every time, from relationship issues to money problems, to health concerns and beyond. You simply cannot feel the Lord work through you without proper and consistent Bible study, prayer, and meditation.

Prayer needs to be treated as a relationship, not a garbage dump. Too often people go to God when something is troubling them and they just unload. Of course God wants believers to come to Him: "Be anxious for nothing, but in everything with prayer and supplication, with thanksgiving, make your requests known to God." (Philippians 4:6) God wants to comfort but a relationship with the Almighty needs to move to the next level. A good friend opens their heart but also their ears. God wants to have a conversation, so spend time merely listening. During prayer time, have conversations with God and in times of meditation and reflection just experience God, be still and in His presence—listen. Of course the Bible must be a consistent partner. The Bible is obviously a key way for God to communicate, so seeking His will must include reading and studying it, exploring the truth of the Bible from cover to cover because all of it is true. Once the foolish decision is made to pick and choose what to believe in the Bible, only a limited relationship with God is possible due to stubborn pride and arrogance.

God wants people to know Him so He will speak to everyone: "Ask, and it will be given to you; seek, and you will find; knock and it will be opened to you." (Matthew 7:7) God always helps and answers the prayers of those who desire to know the Lord more and to achieve perfect faith. Psalm 37:4 says it best: "Delight yourself also in the Lord, and He will give you the desires of your heart." Delighting in the Lord requires aligning your will with His and if the desire is to grow closer to Him, He will be faithful and answer prayers to enable perfect faith.

When seeking God's help, come to Him with a proper attitude. Verses 6–11 exhort believers to come to God with a humble heart. Verse 6 reminds us to "ask in faith, with no doubting" because as His precious children He wants what is best for us. You are special and wonderful and can be confident when spending time with the Almighty. "Let us therefore come boldly to the throne of grace, that we may obtain mercy and find grace to help in time of need." (Hebrews 4:16) Doubt comes from concluding our path is better than God's, placing ourselves ahead of God and putting the corrupted world's values before God's will. Doubt is a product of pride. Verses 9–11 are specifically directed toward those of financial means because they would be particularly prone to relying upon themselves and lacking humility. James warns the rich to not place their faith in their possessions or themselves because "as a flower of the field he will pass away." (verse 10) Humility before God when seeking His will leads to the omnipotent ruler of the universe helping faith blossom. Seek God's guidance with faith and hope, trusting Him and His work.

Perfect faith is only possible through seeking guidance from God in Bible study, prayer and meditation, and trusting His instructions.

Five Questions for Exploration

- Can you devote 30 minutes extra each day for prayer, meditation, and Bible Study? After one month how did your life change as a result?
- How do you show God you want to be His best friend?
- In what ways can you make spending time with God a priority in your daily routine?
- How can you align your desires regarding your trial with God's will?
- In what ways do you place yourself before God? God before you?

THE PATH TO PEACE IS THROUGH THE EAR

3

James 1:12-20 When a trial comes, don't turn away from God but toward Him

Toward the end of church small group, the pastor made the startling revelation one of our members and friends was in the fight of her life battling cancer that had spread throughout her body. We prayed for Tracy, laid hands on her, and tried to speak comforting words. After returning to my seat this awesome calm and confidence come over me, and I just knew in my heart she was going to be fine and make it through this unbelievably difficult trial. After the meeting, Tracy and I had a chance to speak privately and, looking right into her eyes, I told her what was in my heart. A year has passed and her cancer is almost entirely gone. She feels strong and healthy. Her attitude is amazingly uplifting to everyone. During a recent talk, she told me she really had heard my words and believed them, which had given her strength during the many surgeries and treatments. Tracy could have focused on her cancer and shut her ears to what may have seemed like the ridiculous ravings of an idiot when I told her in the absolute depths of her cancer fight she was going to be fine. Instead, she opened her heart and ears. Listening to God, whether He speaks directly to your heart or through another believer, is the path to peace.

Trusting God enough to truly listen to Him means turning toward Him and placing your life in His capable hands, which is the major theme of this section of James. By doing so and by developing perfect faith, you "will receive the crown of life which the Lord has promised to those who love Him." (verse 12) The crown of life *is* the state of perfect faith. Believers can claim this wonderful reward right now by achieving the level of perfect faith, but a failure to seek God blocks any attempt to reach this height of spiritual maturity. When a trial hits, an initial reaction of anger, sadness, or some other negative emotion is perfectly normal, but it is a dangerous time. Turning back to God as quickly as possible is necessary, because destructive temptation will try to creep in and offer a path or solution outside His will during this initial reaction stage. You cannot blame God for those feelings. (verse 13) This enticement isn't centered on alcohol or drugs or sex, but rather on the root cause of those things: "But each one is tempted when he is drawn away by his own desires and enticed." (verse 14) Seeking comfort in something other than God's glory, being self-centered and focused on the problem or selfish desires, will create an opportunity for temptation to lure anyone away from God. Unfortunately, it's a very short step to finding an easy solution in something other than God's will and timing. God requires work while the world offers a quick "fix." Selfishness and damaging impatience are the cause, not God, and "when desire has conceived, it gives birth to sin." (verse 15)

God, on the other hand, is the cause of every good and perfect thing (verses 16–17) and He will move mountains to help you become a better person and grow closer to Him, including giving or allowing trials. It's hard to think of trials as a good thing but never forget the powerful promise of Romans 8:28: "And we know that all things work together for good to those who love God, to those who are called according to His purpose." He loves you and saved you for a reason. He has empowered His precious children to see the world as He sees it and to trust Him for the things they can't see. (verse 18) Believers must turn toward Him and humbly seek His will and obey it, knowing full well infinite God knows far better how to manage trials and emotions than we do.

Those negative emotions don't need to turn someone away from God, but rather the infinite power of God equips us to resist temptation and to throw off those emotions when seeking Him. The number one thing to do is take a breath and listen. In the midst of a trial, "be swift to hear, slow to speak, slow to wrath" (verse 19) because it is impossible to hear God in the midst of yelling and complaining. When faced with a trial, the easy thing to do is fret and vent. God *is* going to speak comforting words and offer perfect guidance. Anger blocks God, closes ears, and consumes the time needed for listening. No good can come of it: "for the wrath of man does not produce the righteousness of God." (verse 20)

I cannot tell you how many times verse 20 has convicted me. Every single time, anger makes things worse. Every time. As soon as my anger flashes, verse 20 runs through my head and the Holy Spirit convicts my heart. My daughter and I have a wonderful relationship, but even we have tough times on occasion. One Saturday I was frustrated about some other things and my eight-year-old decided it was the perfect time to not listen—about anything. Growing angry, my voice rose. She stepped back and ran into her room. Verse 20. Immediately, I opened my heart to the Lord's calming voice.

Entering her room, I spoke to her in an appropriate and helpful way and listened to her with full attention. She felt better and we hugged it out. My anger, clearly outside God's will, produced nothing but trouble. Relying upon God's power made the relationship with my daughter better. If you don't listen to God, you'll never be able to listen to someone else. Taking a breath enables hearing God and calmly reengaging with an appropriate tone and speech, ready to listen. Things will immediately and markedly improve.

To bring this entire section from the beginning of the book to now together, James 1:3 stated, "The testing of your faith produces patience." Listening to God creates the opportunity to be patient. When a trial hits, turn to God, listen to Him, and see the trial for what it is: a beautiful opportunity for God to develop perfect faith, and with it comes incredible joy, peace, and contentment.

Five Questions for Exploration

- During your last trial, did you turn to God or rely upon yourself to solve the problem?
- What are the causes of your trial?
- How does God show you He loves you?
- Do you merely know Romans 8:28 or do you feel it in the depths of your heart?
- What steps can you take to better listen to God?

4

INSIDE AND OUT

James 1:21-James 2:26 - Defense of faith and works and the need for a full commitment

It was one of those days—a long day at work made seemingly longer by a series of situations gone wrong. You know, one of those days where you drop things you normally wouldn't, trip on invisible carpet threads, and stumble over important words when you really can't afford to do so. I came home to a sink full of dishes. I hate coming home to a sink full of dishes. In the midst of washing a glass I didn't want to wash, my wife harmlessly asked me to keep it down. My anger, which was already evident in the needless clanging of plates and bowls, boiled over. Melissa lovingly asked what was wrong but I didn't hear her words and launched my frustration at her. My conduct did not match my character, as I had let circumstances guide my actions instead of the Lord.

After establishing the fundamental truth trials have the godly purpose of developing perfect faith when you turn to God and listen, James transitions in this section to the other side of the coin: the outward manifestation of matured, perfect faith. He begins Chapter 1:21 with "Therefore" to denote a conclusion and change of thought. Just as James correctly concluded in the first section of the book anger serves as a roadblock to listening to God, he further concludes sin will have the same result (verse 21). Sin separates us from God, even though it cannot separate us from His love. Everyone sins, everyone falls short of God's perfection—the Almighty knows this and understands. He also cannot abide sin, which is why God works so hard to help His children get better. Keeping the focus on glorifying God lessens sinful disobedience. We will falter and make poor decisions, but the key is to turn to Him and let the Holy Spirit work through you to do better the next time. Stubbornly clutching to sins makes it impossible to hear God. The more life revolves around sin, the less likely you will "receive with meekness the implanted word." (verse 21)

As faith grows, conduct must match it; we must "be doers of the word." (verse 22) Maturing faith which does not manifest itself in right conduct becomes a superficial spiritual walk, like a man who looks at his face in a mirror and then forgets (verses 23–24). His relationship with his own reflection, with his own nature, would be so surface as to leave no lasting impression. Immersion in the word of God and the conduct to match it, however, will result in blessings (verse 25). Verse 25 suggests the believer would look intently and study the word and God's will (Walvoord, 1983). The person who does this would develop a deep faith (perfect faith). Verse 25 mentions the "perfect law of liberty." God's law is perfect, and abiding by it and in it sets one free. Conduct reflecting this freedom would make a committed believer a true light on the world.

Right character expresses itself in right conduct (verses 26–27). This is the essence of James's defense of faith and works. A fully committed believer immerses himself or herself in both God's word and will in order to develop an ever more faithful heart, and at the same time the believer's conduct reflects this progression. Verse 27 mentions "pure and undefiled religion" and specifically gives the example of visiting "orphans and widows in their trouble." This should not be taken to reflect an exhaustive list or to suggest a checklist. The reference here is to right conduct generally. The verse also mentions "to keep oneself unspotted from the world." This refers to right character. The inseparable forces of the inside and the outside, the heart and the action, are both necessary to lead a fully committed Christian walk.

Chapter 2:1–13 expands on the previous point. "My brethren, do not hold the faith of our Lord Jesus Christ, the Lord of glory, with partiality." (verse 1) Walk into a room and turn on the light. The light does not bend of its own free will and only illuminate a certain corner of the room, but rather the light illuminates everything to the best of its ability. Faith shines in the same way. Your light will illuminate everything around you to the best of its ability according to how brightly you shine. James implores us not to dispense our faith in a discriminating manner, only giving it to those we favor or from whom we want something. Being fully committed means doing the hard work of showing courtesy to everyone. Believers must avoid giving the best places of their lives only to those who are rich or powerful or famous (verses 2–3). Certainly, this can extend to those who are kind; Jesus modeled the behavior of being wonderfully courteous to the unkind or those who have done wrong just as much as to those who are friends. If right conduct only extends to those who look the part or who act according to preconceived notions, have we not merely "become judges with evil thoughts?" (verse 4) Are you courteous to everyone or only to those who look or act a certain way?

Honestly, I'm not much of a road rager. I genuinely try to drive at a normal speed and enjoy the ride—unless I need to get somewhere by a specific time and the clock is ticking. Circumstances quite often get the better of me. On the road during those times, when someone shows me kindness I'm all smiles, but if someone cuts me off then hell hath no fury. If my conduct truly matched my character, if I truly had perfect faith in this area of my life, I would treat both circumstances with the same kindness. I'm working on it. Right conduct doesn't come and go like a feather in the wind depending on the circumstances. Right conduct born of perfect faith is an absolute rock failing to be swayed by the vagaries of the day. How consistent are you with your courtesy?

In addition to being courteous to all, we should be compassionate to all (verses 5–7). Don't show disdain for those who are poor or who are not as financially successful. We live in a world that values selfishness and greed hidden under the dark cloak of financial success. Society tells us to get more and more money and possessions, to acquire financial power and all the toys that come with it. So it is natural to run the rat race and compare ourselves to those who don't run as fast or as far. From comparison it is a short leap to judgment. It may be natural to do so, but it is neither right nor acceptable to God, whose love is all-consuming. He doesn't merely love part of you, so don't be partial showing love to others, for "if you show partiality, you commit sin." (verse 9)

James spends the next several verses (10–13) expounding on the seriousness of partiality. Partial obedience is disobedience and James even uses the extreme examples of adultery and murder to prove the point (verse 11). If someone does not commit adultery but does commit murder, he still has transgressed by committing murder. God doesn't use scales of justice to weigh sins. For those who would make light of courtesy and compassion to all, James warns failing to do so is a serious breach. A godly heart must reveal itself in right conduct to all.

In verse 14 he uses the phrase "my brethren" to suggest a point of emphasis as he concludes this major section of the book. In verses 14–26 James continues in the theme of money to address the need for works to be the manifestation of faith. Just as it does no good (and in fact is a sin) to show favoritism to the wealthy, it does not "profit" to have right character and not right conduct. James asks the question, "Can faith save him?" (verse 14) Be careful here. Remember the purpose of the book of James is NOT to expound on salvation but rather to explain how growing faith should reveal itself and as such the word "faith" here in the question posed by James refers to insincere faith and not whether faith is present. In verses 15–16 James in essence gives the clue by immediately answering the question with an illustration of a destitute man and a believer's response, which is to do nothing. Having faith but doing nothing does not profit the world or as James rhetorically asks at the end of verse 16, "What does it profit?" James starts verse 17 with "Thus" to suggest a conclusion of the previous verses 14–16. He proclaims: "Thus also faith by itself, if it does not have works, is dead." Again, he is not saying works are required for salvation; the gift of grace is an unearned and unmerited gift of salvation by God. In no way do you have to rise to some standard of right conduct to claim the gift of grace. He is saying faith should be visible in conduct. This is James calling believers to real action. The Christian faith is an activist one requiring conscious and deliberate effort to seek the Lord's will, to pray, read the Bible, and meditate on the Word, but also to act differently than the rest of the world as a light to the world. It is a faith functioning as salt and light (Matthew 5:13), which means it must express itself in outward action impacting the world. The inner change of heart needs to express itself in an outward change of conduct.

The mysterious someone enters the picture in verse 18. Here James is using a hypothetical conversation to illustrate the point of the need for faith and works to have a fully committed Christian walk. The "someone" is declaring they don't need faith because they have works. James hypothetically responds: take away your works and your lack of faith is exposed, but "I will show you my faith by my works." Just as outward good conduct without inward faith is useless and superficial, inward faith without outward good conduct reveals a life falling short of the wonderful plan God has for you.

James then drives home the point by highlighting three examples. Believing in one God doesn't create some enlightened person worthy of praise because even "demons believe." (verse 19) Abraham, the great Jewish patriarch, revealed his faith by taking action "when he offered Isaac his son on the altar." (verse 21) His faith was made perfect (or in other words complete) because his strong faith was manifested in faithful right conduct (verse 22). Outside of Jesus, has there ever been a clearer example of perfect faith than Abraham's actions on the altar? (Genesis 22:1–19) Finally, Rahab revealed her faith "when she received the messengers and sent them out another way." (verse 25)

In each of these examples the temptation might be to muddy the waters by seeing these as statements of the need for works in order to gain salvation. Justification is used often in these passages. To be justified is to be declared righteous by God when placing faith in the Risen Lord Jesus Christ (see, for example, Romans 3:24). When Paul in the book of Romans uses the word "justification," he is referring to salvation; when James uses justification, his emphasis is on salvation being revealed by actions (Walvoord, 1983). Abraham, who obviously existed well before the incarnation of Jesus Christ, could not therefore be justified by faith in Christ, but his justification was still revealed by his faithful conduct. Verse 22 places this section and particularly verse 24 in proper context: "Do you see that faith was working together with his works, and by works faith was made perfect?" His emphasis is on the fact faith and works should go together in a person's life to reveal a complete commitment to God. Seen in this light, verse 24 reiterates those twin forces rather than contradicts them: "You see then that a man is justified by works, and not by faith only." (verse 24) Conduct, while not earning salvation, reveals a person's inner transformation. James is railing against useless faith failing to produce changed conduct. He is criticizing those who merely profess their faith and who do not by consequence have a fully committed Christian life.

James closes the section on the following concluding statement: "For as the body without the spirit is dead, so faith without works is dead also." (verse 26) A human body without a spirit has no purpose, no inner sense of self. It is merely skin and bones without real existence. With regard to the higher and more important aspects of life it is useless. If faith does not reveal itself in good conduct it is unused, it is like a covered light illuminating nothing (Matthew 5:15). A fully committed Christian walk occurs when a believer seeks perfect faith in all areas of his or her life and when maturing faith manifests in consistent right conduct.

Five Questions for Exploration

- What sin in your life is keeping you from hearing God?
- In what ways does your conduct match your character?
- In what ways does your conduct fall short of your character?

- In what ways do you fall short of being courteous to everyone and what practical steps can you take to address that?
- In what ways do you fall short of being compassionate to everyone and what practical steps can you take to address that?

A GODLY HEART
SAYS NICE THINGS

5

James 3 - A fully committed Christian walk
includes a godly heart

While having lunch at a local fast food restaurant, I suddenly became aware this was the best fast food hamburger I had ever had. Looking around the restaurant and noticing its cleanliness, I remembered the kindness of the cashier and decided to do something very unusual for me. Going back up to the counter and asking to see the manager resulted in the cashier's face dropping in disappointment. The manager was busy so the cashier called over the assistant manager, who was behind me working at a table doing some paperwork. The assistant manager walked up to me carefully, and without a word from me, asked in a dejected tone with slumped shoulders: "What's wrong?" I reassured her nothing was amiss and actually wanted to commend her on running such a wonderful restaurant with such delicious hamburgers. It was as if doves had lifted off my shoulders and angels descended upon me. She was so grateful she called the manager out from the back and had me retell the glorious story. Before we parted the assistant manager said something I have never forgotten. She leaned in and said "You don't know how much this means to me; I've had such a hard week." A hard week. How beaten down had she become from the parade of people complaining? Not a hard day, but a hard week. It was only Wednesday. How had her dejected attitude at work impacted her home life or those people she came across in her normal daily routine? Now I have no idea, but I like to think maybe her day was a little better and maybe when she went home she smiled a little more at her husband or kids, but ever since then I have made a point of carrying blank thank-you cards in my car and, when receiving exemplary service, make a point of asking for the manager and hand the note over with some extra words of appreciation. I have often gone back to one of the places and seen my note hanging on the wall.

After establishing the indispensable link between character and conduct in the previous major section of the book, in Chapter 3 James explores how a godly heart leads to right speech. Beginning with Chapter 3 and continuing on for the rest of the book, he emphasizes the heart and what it can and should produce. It is only fitting that he does so. The entire book began with James exploring how trials can help a believer develop perfect faith. He then connected that with conduct. A believer's Christian walk must begin with the careful cultivation of the heart, the inner man, but it must include the outward walk, how we as believers interact with the world around us. The rest of the book should be taken as expanded comments regarding the link between right character and right conduct.

Verse 1 starts with the common refrain, "My brethren," which again suggests the reader should notice a change in topic, and indeed Chapter 3 is focused almost exclusively on one of the central challenges of the believer's life: speech. The first verse may seem out of place or thrown in because seemingly out of left field James suggests the dangers of being a teacher, but it actually makes perfect sense within the flow of the narrative. Numerous verses in the Bible remind believers the more God gives the more He expects. With greater responsibility certainly comes greater expectations. Jesus explicitly declared: "For everyone to whom much is given, from him much will be required; and to whom much has been committed, of him they will ask the more." (Luke 12:48) Teachers have great responsibility and obviously much is expected. James is playfully suggesting he doesn't envy those who have great responsibility and expectations because "we all stumble in many things" and one of the primary reasons for falling short of those expectations is when we "stumble in word." (verse 2)

James spends verses 3–5 providing various examples of how little things can have incredible consequences. An entire horse is guided by a small bit (verse 3), a large ship is turned by a tiny rudder (verse 4), and a great forest can be brought to ash by a little fire (verse 5). How often have you seen a small thing have terrible and unexpected consequences? Speech can most assuredly be a fire, "a world of iniquity" (verse 6), destroying a believer's witness. Humans can harness almost innumerable aspects of the physical environment, we can explore space and the ocean deep, but that tiny little tongue defies efforts to control it (verses 7–8). "But no man can control the tongue. It is an unruly evil, full of deadly poison." (verse 8) Speech is capable of inspiring but also of destroying (verses 9–10), and we are all guilty of the latter. It can wound, manipulate, belittle, and do a hundred other negative things. The terrible reality is the wounds we make with words have far more lasting effect than the words we use to build up.

While we are painfully inconsistent with our speech, sometimes positively impacting people and other times hurting them, "these things ought not to be so." (verse 10) In fact, the incongruity of both building people up with words and tearing them down with the same mouth is unnatural for a believer who has Jesus Christ in their heart. Just as a spring cannot send forth both fresh and bitter water (verse 11) or a fig tree bring forth olives (verse 12), a fully committed believer who has developed perfect faith would so allow the beauty of the Holy Spirit to flow through them, out to the world only positive, edifying speech would pour from their mouths.

The key, as always, is the source, and James delves into the topic in verses 13–18 to end the chapter. A spring can bring forth fresh or salt water (verse 12) but it depends on the source. The believer's foundation is the Lord Jesus Christ. A godly heart seeks the Lord's counsel and puts Him first by stepping out of the way to let the Holy Spirit do His work. Good speech is "done in the meekness of wisdom." (verse 13) A wise person understands the need to submit to God as a servant by seeking the Lord's will and obeying it. Abiding in godly wisdom is the source of consistently positive speech.

Trouble comes when we place ourselves first. Envious and selfish hearts deny the truth of godly wisdom (verse 14). Envy and selfishness are not from God but are products of the world's twisted and "demonic" values (verse 15), and where those two reside "confusion and every evil thing are there." (verse 16) In contrast to the selfishness of the world's values, "the wisdom that is from above is first pure, then peaceable, gentle, willing to yield, full of mercy and good fruits, without partiality and without hypocrisy." (verse 17) Godly wisdom is consistently truthful, uplifting, compassionate, kind, and without blemish. A wise heart desires peace; a fully committed believer uses his or her speech to produce the fruit of peace (verse 18).

In Chapter 2 James declared right character should express itself in things such as courtesy and compassion to all. He extended the idea in Chapter 3 to pronounce right character also should reveal itself in right speech to all. Right character (developing perfect faith) results in right conduct (positive speech). Speech can build up or tear down because words have a powerful effect. On our own we cannot control the tongue, but with the wisdom of the Lord in our heart we will use words to be peacemakers and to produce good fruit.

Five Questions for Exploration

- What practical steps can you implement so God can trust you with more spiritual responsibility?
- Describe an experience where your words uplifted someone.
- Describe an experience where your words hurt someone.
- Is your speech a product of your circumstances or a God-centered heart?
- Take one month and make an effort to send handwritten thank-you notes. Describe your experience. How did it heighten your spiritual journey?

HUMILITY IS POWER

6

James 4 - A godly heart is a humble heart

A few years ago I was in a position—family, house, nice neighborhood, possessions – suddenly threatened by an unexpected job loss. Praying to God for Him to provide a new job (and stupidly reminding God how important it is to provide for family), the very next day a company called to schedule an interview and ended up offering a position. Problem solved—or so I thought. Bills could now be paid but I absolutely hated the job and eventually quit. Praying once again for a job (but a nicer one), the very next day the phone rang again for an interview and eventually that job came through. Better, but the Holy Spirit began to tug on my heart as a sense of unease crept in so I prayed for guidance, but this time focused on God's will and not my own. I was sitting in my car praying to God and spending time with Him, focused solely on using the spiritual gifts He had given me. If God blessed me with an avenue to do so, I would welcome the opportunity. The word "opportunity" still hung in the air when the phone rang. Fifteen minutes later my dream school offered a fantastic job. Putting myself first resulted in

OK, but humbly placing God ahead of my problem and focusing on His glory produced the best possible outcome.

The major thrust of Chapter 4 is the importance of humbly setting aside your selfish desires to focus on God's will. After ending Chapter 3 on the obligation of believers to be peacemakers via their wisdom in seeking God's will, James naturally starts Chapter 4 with an examination of the root of strife. After all, it is one thing to understand your role as a peacemaker and something else to successfully navigate real-world situations. Much of Chapter 3 was consumed by the pitfalls of speech, especially when it comes from a self-centered heart. Words from a godly heart can absolutely uplift and inspire but in order to hit the right message, a believer has to understand why conflict is present.

Certainly, conflict can seem to be a very complex thing because we tend to weave multiple issues into a situation, but James strikes right at the heart of the matter and offers an insightful look into the human mind. James begins the chapter with an obligatory question: "Where do wars and fights come from among you?" (verse 1) He immediately offers a question as answer: "Do they not come from your desires for pleasure that war in your members?" The truth of the question certainly convicts every one of us, and there is no need for James to answer because we know it to be true. Our greed, avarice, lust, self-indulgence, and a whole host of other ungodly desires compete against each other for their self-appointed place in our lives. A twisted milieu of selfish desires causes inner turmoil and poor decisions, and such tension and stress expresses itself in strife with others. When we look at the history of the world, the presence of conflict jumps out. Throughout history the desire for land has been the greatest cause of conflict because historically it has been the measure of economic success. Even in these urban-centric times within our industrial system, precious resources make the world go round and we create unnecessary and terrible conflict to acquire them. In crowded areas, the need for viable living space causes conflict as we scratch and claw for every square inch or neighborhood block. The Mideast conflict is a classic example of how we add things to our desires and make the situation muddled. The essence of the conflicts in that region is space. Religion and culture, often portrayed in the media as the central causes (especially religion), are but political footballs used by those who wish to further a political agenda centered on land. The reason why the efforts at peace always fail is because there is a conscious effort to not strike at the real heart of the matter: the desire for land and all that comes with it in terms of perceived economic viability and power. It boils down to greed and such a thing does not come from God but from selfish desires. God calls on believers to be humble, and humility has no room for greed. Humility is in fact the opposite of greed.

The folly of man is we know greed is ungodly and yet we still cling to it like grim death. Even though God consistently and constantly demands humility in money and possessions, the selfish desire for such things takes precedence. We count the depth of our offerings by how much we give, not how much we have left. James reminds us greed is an illusion, a trap (verse 2). The next thing desired stays just beyond the fingertips and so the fruitless efforts on the rat wheel end up signifying nothing. When dreams revolve around money and possessions, lives are doomed to disappoint. Money will never bring true joy; possessions will never result in validation; addiction will never lead to peace. All these are paths of the world, all these will fail to deliver, so seemingly two choices remain: either be unhappy and in despair or rationalize away unhappiness and despair to declare the lie of success. Of course a third path exists: recognize God is the source of true joy, peace, and contentment, and understand the need to seek and serve His will rather than your own.

"You lust and you do not have. You murder and covet and cannot obtain. You fight and war. Yet you do not have because you do not ask." (verse 2) Because we cannot possess the things we lust after or obtain the things coveted, tension ensues—conflict is the product of selfish desires. The very nature of lust and covetousness is also a false idol because acquiring the thing desired means it no longer holds any interest and instead the mind switches gear and is consumed by the fear of keeping it. My wife's former car is a classic example of the fear. Her dream car was always a Mazda Miata, a little roadster. A few years ago for our anniversary I bought her the car and surprised her at work one day over lunch. She was so excited. One of her great passions is to shop but now she had a car too nice to receive door dings. During trips to the mall she always parked as far away as possible at the far end of the lot. Inevitably, when it was time to leave another car was parked right next to her precious Miata even though there were other empty spaces all around. Wherever she went constant worry followed her. The stress was so great she had to sell her dream car. When we desire earthly pleasures we stress about getting and keeping. Verse 2 is not suggesting, though, to ask God for the self-centered desires.

Selfish desires come from a lack of true clarity as the world defines goals and ambitions, which is the road to despair. It is also without common sense. The world system is antithetical to God's plan. Everything the world holds dear—money, possessions, power, fame, celebrity, entitlement—is contrary to God. God desires humility and intimacy; the sovereign, omnipotent ruler of the universe wants to be your best friend. Godly goals cannot exist unless God controls the nature and form. Do you define your goals or does God? Most people fall far short of the mark because they let the world define their dreams, but here in verse 2 James is calling on believers to make the effort to ask God and let Him determine the parameters of life. Desire for a possession will always disappoint because it can't deliver what is promised and conflict will exist to get it and keep it. A God-defined goal will never disappoint because almighty God wants to grow your faith.

The key is: Do you ask for God to grant the possession or do you ask God to help faith grow? "You ask and do not receive, because you ask amiss, that you may spend it on your pleasures." (verse 3) God may or may not give you what you want, but He will always give you what you need. What is truly needed in this life is the one thing He wants: to grow closer to Him by growing in your faith. When faced with a trial, the natural thing to do is ask God to fix the problem. Confronted with the loss of a job, for example, the temptation is to ask God for another one because fear consumes the mind and concerns about bills and responsibilities flood in—the focus is on possessions and status. Asking God to bless you with money and material things is not the path to perfect faith, and it also limits God to only giving what *you* see as good. Do you want what is good, what is better, or what is best? God wants what is best for you. If focus is on the world's definition of success, settling for good is all that will ever come; center your request on God's will and He provides His best. As James bluntly puts it: "Adulterers and adulteresses! Do you now know that friendship with the world is enmity with God? Whoever therefore wants to be a friend of the world makes himself an enemy of God." (verse 4) It is impossible to serve two masters; you cannot desire the world's warped definition of success and God's perfect definition of success. This is precisely what so many Christians today want to do, and this is why they have a very limited walk with God and are either all twisted inside with stress or have compromised their faith to the point where God's will means little to nothing in a dogged pursuit of the world's pleasures. The path to peace and security isn't through the tangled web of self or the twisted soul of society but rather down the illuminated trial blazed by God. Only through God's will is it possible to live an extraordinary life.

True power, victory, and success are found in God and not the world (verses 5–6). If you want a great marriage, ask God to enter it and let Him be the guide. If you want a wonderfully fulfilling job, ask God to put you in a position to glorify Him by using your spiritual gifts. A person who makes $1 furthering God's kingdom is worth infinitely more than the person who makes $1 million furthering himself. James reaches the conclusion in verse 7 with his customary "Therefore." You must "submit to God. Resist the devil and he will flee from you." Take action by humbling yourself and submitting to God's will. To submit to God, put away selfish desires (and thereby strife with God and fellow man) and come closer to God by seeking His will; by doing so He will be there for you and "draw near to you." (verse 8) Growing closer to God by obeying His will means one must inherently move away from sin because God cannot abide sin (verse 8). Recognize sinful desires block you from experiencing God's best. Humility means understanding God knows better; sin is placing desires ahead of God. Putting God ahead of sinful desires turns the universe upside down and what used to give temporary feelings of happiness no longer hold the same sway. We like to revel in worldly success but once true humility before God exists, pursuing the world's path is no cause for happiness (verse 9). True joy—joy that exists whether good or bad things happen—comes through developing perfect faith in obedience to God's will; true peace comes from taking action to further God's kingdom. What the world calls powerless—humility—is actually the greatest power one can wield. The world will try to manipulate and destroy because godliness threatens its very existence, but humble "yourselves in the sight of the Lord, and He will lift you up." (verse 10)

Humility before God leads to humility with neighbors—a point connecting this section not only to the very beginning of the chapter when James explored the root of strife but also to Chapter 3's emphasis on speech. A humble believer does not place himself or herself on God's level by judging others (verses 11–12). Pride and arrogance—tools of the world system—reveal themselves when assuming such an exalted position. Jesus declared: "Judge not, that you be not judged." (Matthew 7:1) Some might misinterpret this declaration as a defense of moral relativism—it is not. Jesus did not say we should avoid uplifting someone by helping them recognize where they fall short, but He did say interaction with a fallen believer needs to be from a place of love, humility, and spiritual maturity: "First remove the plank from your own eye, and then you will see clearly to remove the speck from your brother's eye." (Matthew 7:5) In other words, rather than rush to tell someone what they should do, kneel humbly before God and let Him reveal how to live your life and grow in faith. James is working along the same line of thought. A humble heart cannot judge others because it recognizes its own meekness and the need for God in its life. Words reveal the heart: speech filled with judgment comes from a heart filled with arrogance, but words filled with encouragement and love come from a humble, godly heart. Only God can judge: "There is one Lawgiver, who is able to save and to destroy. Who are you to judge another?" (verse 12)

Just as words can be used to tear down others through judgment, boasts deny a witness and reveal a prideful heart (verses 13–14). Boasting about accomplishments isn't confined to aggressive blowhards reminding everyone in the room how much they're worth. It can be as subtle as the little twinge when seeing a homeless person or the impulse to define success by keeping up with the Joneses. On a recent trip to the grocery store, I drove behind a guy driving this very expensive convertible. His license plate read "U Can 2." The boastful implication from the top of his pedestal was clear: if I follow his path I can be as successful, I can reach his heights. Boasting reveals pleasure in things. A humble person doing the will of God finds no pleasure in possessing things but rather finds joy in recognizing everything one has is from God and can be taken away by God. We are merely stewards of the blessings God allows us to have. Certain possessions don't define success; a successful life is determined by a growing relationship with the Lord, which is only possible enveloped in humility before Him. God doesn't smile when you buy the latest shiny thing, but rather when embracing the obedient servant's role. So much of existence in this world is wrapped up in planning and thinking about the future and what that will look like. These visions never center on living under a bridge homeless, but, rather, they bloom with educational success leading to economic prosperity and a house, car, vacations, and toys. Such is the path of folly because "you will not know what will happen tomorrow." (verse 14) The Lord Jesus Christ proclaims, "Do not worry about tomorrow, for tomorrow will worry about its own things. Sufficient for the day is its own trouble." (Matthew 6:34) Treasures hoarded here on earth have no value in Heaven (Matthew 6:19–20). Focusing on acquiring money and possessions reveals a world-centered and self-centered heart. "For where your treasure is, there your heart will be also." (Matthew 6:21) Boasting, then, serves no good purpose. It reveals a prideful heart and can't possibly lead to fulfillment. To boast causes stress and strife and tears others down by placing one person above another. It reveals a fool: "For what is your life? It is even a vapor that appears for a little time and then vanishes away." (verse 14) Our time here on earth is an infinitesimally small speck compared to the infinite vastness of time believers exist in Heaven, yet we spend so much of it worried about getting and keeping and what others have and want. All such things are a terrible waste of time because what we have or will have is up to God, and a God-centered life revolves around doing His will, not possessions or status: "Instead you ought to say, 'If the Lord wills, we shall live and do this or that.'" (verse 15) A humble heart is a godly heart which places itself under the protection and guidance of God. It is a servant's heart where the only master it serves is the Lord Jesus Christ. A boastful heart wallows in greed and puts on airs of gloating to hide its own self-loathing. "All such boasting is evil." (verse 16)

James ends Chapter 4 in the customary way with a conclusion: "Therefore, to him who knows to do good and does not do it, to him it is sin." (verse 17) Believers know what they should do: cultivate a humble heart by submitting to the will of God in clear recognition He knows best. We should speak from the humility of our hearts and never judge or boast or cause strife, but rather help, feel compassion, and make peace. To do otherwise is to disobey God by committing sin.

Five Questions for Exploration

- How have your desires caused conflict?
- Do you ask God for your earthly desires, or do you ask God to help you grow in your faith?
- Would your friends say your master is the world or God? Is their perception based on how you live your life?

- In what ways do you humble yourself before God to draw closer to Him?
- In what subtle or explicit ways do you boast and what impact does that have on your testimony?

A SERVANT'S HEART IS THE PATH TO LIVING IN PERFECT FAITH

7

James 5 - A humble heart patiently seeks God's will through consistent, committed prayer

Mom lay on the bed with closed eyes struggling through horrific death breaths. Her chest heaved up and down with every terrible attempt. She was home now, having spent much of the previous few weeks in the hospital. There, with two of my sisters and Debra the nurse, I knew what I had to do, so I left the room to pray in solitude. It wasn't the first time a fateful decision had fallen on my shoulders. While in the hospital, the doctors confirmed she had a massive and growing tumor in her brain. They gave me the choice of surgery to remove it or take her home. Seeking guidance from the Holy Spirit, I understood with crystal clarity my mom would rather live out her remaining days at home than suffer through a post-surgery lifestyle. A week later as she lay on her couch unable to move, the Holy Spirit moved me to pray over her, feebly communicate how much I loved her, and tell her she was going to die. She had lost the ability to speak but I saw clearly in her eyes she understood. I'll never forget those eyes. As I knelt in prayer that fateful night, alone with God, my heart knew I had to release any selfish desire and focus solely on being a servant to God's will and my mom. Walking back into the room with a confidence that only comes from humble submission to God's will and with a peace that only comes from the absolute knowledge life is in service to God and others, I came to her bedside. Gathered around the bed, holding hands with Debra and my sisters, I prayed for God to call my precious momma home that night. He did so at 3:30 a.m.

In the midst of this trial my personal journey through James had come to fruition. Six years before, I lay curled up in a ball on my bathroom floor crying uncontrollably out of fear and stress and sadness, worried about my cancer and how my wife and daughter would live without me. At that point I was just setting out on the long path to perfect faith. While praying over my mother, I faced the moment with a calm confidence and peace born only of an intimacy with God, absolute submission to His will, and utter service to my so very precious momma. I was able to face the moment with strength precisely because I had embraced God's purpose during my previous trials and worked to develop perfect faith.

The ultimate focus of Chapter 5 is the power and significance of prayer and service to others, which is the epicenter of living in perfect faith. James begins by continuing his previous discussion of humility as he launches Chapter 5 with an elegant and biting refutation of one of his favorite punching bags: misguided wealth. It is important to note James does not take issue with wealth itself, which is similar to Paul's statement in his letter to Timothy: "For the love of money is a root of all kinds of evil, for which some have strayed in their greediness, and pierced themselves through with many arrows." (1 Timothy 6:10) The lust for money brings forth the evil—money is merely a tool without any significance other than what humans attach to it. This is the very thing James is protesting: placing value on wealth, boasting about it, glorifying the acquisition of wealth, and thereby placing it on a pedestal even ahead of God to the point where it decimates your testimony and witness as a child of God.

"Come now, you rich, weep and howl for your miseries that are coming upon you!" (verse 1) James here is cutting the wealthy down to size. As a product of the human condition in the frailty and foolishness of our minds, too often we uphold the wealthy and esteem them better than the rest of us folk. After all, according to the world's values, they have the most valuable things: economic and social power. They ride in nicer cars and have bigger homes. They experience life on a different level and have access to opportunities others simply do not possess. Such a view looks at wealth from within the prism of the world's twisted value system. James actually pities the wealthy and by doing so casts a bright light on the folly of wealth and those who pursue it. Rather than being glorified, James portrays the wealthy as wallowing in misery with more miseries soon to come. Instead of boasting, the wealthy should weep and howl. "Your riches are corrupted, and your garments are moth-eaten." (verse 2) Wealth doesn't imbue someone with greater moral fiber or character. It doesn't make a person better or one inch closer to God. Riches cannot because their very nature is corrupted by ungodly human pursuit, so in fact the pursuit of wealth pushes one away from God. The more time consumed pursuing wealth, the less time one has for pursuing God. Money doesn't add time to your day.

Wealth manifests itself in objects, including, of course, clothing. Typically, the more money someone has, the finer and more expensive the clothes. James portrays this wealth marker as nothing more than moth-eaten. Some of the most horrifying scenes of the world system are the red carpet celebrity events. The clothing and styling of the celebrities who walk the red carpet are dissected and analyzed by millions around the world. These celebrities are held up as stars, something that lives above us mean folk who walk the earth. They have wealth, fame, and notoriety. They have everything we are supposed to want according to the world's values. James would remind believers those $10,000 designer dresses on the red carpet are but rags-in-waiting, without any real value or merit, and certainly not born of a humble and godly heart. This is not the domain of the rich only. Walk into any clothing store and you see the latest fashion, the promptings to buy, the push to be modern, up-to-date, progressive, cool, whatever. The clothing desired so badly is all soon to be rags and moth-eaten (verse 2). Of course James is using clothing as a tool to prove the point: we fail when we treasure our possessions. Golf is my favorite sport. There's something so beautiful in walking off the first tee after a good drive down the middle of the fairway as the morning dew glistens in the sun and the freshly cut grass sends this wonderful aroma through the air. It's a sport of honor where you penalize yourself. Respect and proper behavior are prized and expected. When I go into a golf store, the beautiful bags and latest clubs beckon. I want them. I would love a membership at an exclusive country club I'll never be able to afford. Folly. All rags.

Money isn't something to be treasured or marveled at because riches are corroded (verse 3). The golden halls are tarnished. What's more, the very corroded wealth itself, while having no value apart from what humans ascribe to it, "will be a witness against you and will eat your flesh like fire." (verse 4) Hoarded wealth, pursued so doggedly, consuming so much time and effort and coming at great cost, actually lessens a believer's testimony. It weakens your relationship with the Lord. Rather than making the spiritual light shine brighter, hoarded wealth in reality dims it.

Jesus Christ called on all believers to be salt and light, to preserve the Word as salt and to be light illuminating the world with God's love, casting aside the darkness of the world system. Jesus was obviously referring to a believer's impact on the world. Hoarding wealth and interacting with friends, acquaintances, and strangers out of a selfish heart lessens your light and harms others. "Indeed the wages of the laborers who mowed your fields, which you kept back by fraud, cry out." (verse 4) This does not only apply to the rich and powerful. Selfish pursuits cause negative consequences for others, and God hears the lamentations of the oppressed (verse 4). While you acquire and hoard, others suffer (verses 5–6).

James astutely concludes in verse 7: "Be patient, brethren, until the coming of the Lord." Treasures acquired on earth are useless; doing God's will enables infinite joy with treasures stored up in Heaven magnified by the glory of God. Being self-centered harms others; being God-centered brings peace and joy to others as you light up the world. It makes no logical sense, then, to put so much emphasis on the things desired for the here and now, yet here we are living a life God never intended us to live pursuing our own glorification. So where's the exit ramp from the rat wheel? James hits on an important and clever connection between the pursuit of wealth and impatience. Pursuit is a product of failing to wait for God's timing. Being perfect in Heaven is the real glory; the truly valuable possessions exist there. Time here on earth is but a single drop of water in an infinite ocean, and while life is a blessing given by God, of course, God always blesses with the intent we use it to bless others. This is true whether it is money, talent, time, or life. Our lives need to be refocused on the goal of patiently serving others. Let God direct your life according to

His timing and will, and bless according to His plan. Truly embracing service will radically change lives, and the more service penetrates down to the smallest detail, the closer to God you become. The life of service is the path to an amazingly extraordinary life. To refocus on others requires the patience to set aside selfish desires and wait on someone else. True patience requires full recognition of a fundamental fact: money and possessions acquired here on earth no longer hold any influence over your life.

When doggedly pursuing earthly desires you will fail to exhibit patience. The essence of James's main point for the entire book—the need for character and conduct—is clear here. The proof is in the act: conduct reveals true character. What do you really pursue during the day? Certainly God blesses us with work, but the point is how imbalanced life is between work or worldly pleasures and God. Add up how much of your day is consumed by work—getting ready, commuting to and from, the actual job, escaping its pressures through entertainment, decompressing from it, etc.—and the time spent with God must pale in comparison. My challenge to you is to take one week and honestly make an inventory of how you spend the days. At the end of the week compare the hours spent on work-related activities or entertainment-based pursuits to the time spent growing closer to your Lord and Savior. Then consciously find more time to spend with the Lord to create a better life balance. It's easier said than done and it most likely will require tough choices and trust in the Lord. You'll be better for it.

James has come full circle from Chapter 1:3, "knowing that the testing of your faith produces patience." He began the book discussing the God-centered purpose of trials and how they serve as opportunities to grow in faith by allowing them to produce patience. Here in Chapter 5:7 James identifies patience, the very thing trials produce, as the key to leading a more fulfilled and meaningful life making the world a better place. Trials, serving their godly purpose of developing perfect faith, will enable your spiritual light to shine brighter. Positively impacting the world through word and deed, peacemaking comes from being a giver, not a taker.

What follows are several lessons from James regarding patience. Just as a farmer ruins his crops by impatiently harvesting them too soon, a believer must patiently wait for the Lord's blessings (verses 7–8). Be aware, however: while waiting for blessings, a believer must actively cultivate a godly heart and to do so with a sense of urgency, "for the coming of the Lord is at hand." (verse 8) The time of the Lord's return is unknown; therefore, do not get caught with an impatient, selfish heart producing strife (verse 9). This may seem like a daunting task, but take heart and look at Job's interaction with the Lord (verses 10–11). Job modeled how to persevere during a trial with patience, but, even more importantly, God demonstrated His compassion and mercy with Job. Finally, a humble, patient heart does not need to boast or swear oaths (verse 12). James here is reiterating almost word for word a statement by Jesus during His Sermon on the Mount: "But let your 'Yes' be 'Yes,' and your 'No,' 'No.' For whatever is more than these is from the evil one." (Matthew 5:33) Just as Jesus in the Sermon on the Mount declares a godly heart does not need to swear oaths, James concludes his section on patience by reminding believers of the same thing. A believer speaking from the power of a patient, humble heart only needs to say yes or no and not embellish those answers with extraneous and pretentious oaths; in fact, doing so reveals a boastful, self-centered heart.

Turning from selfish desires to godly ones, from destructive speech to uplifting words, is a process that begins with consistent and constant prayer. Throughout the book James calls on believers to seek the Lord. In Chapter 1 James implored believers to ask God for help in successfully using trials to develop perfect faith. Chapter 2 reminds people of faith a God-centered heart does not show partiality. In Chapter 3 James goes to great lengths to describe the destructive nature of speech and how only through God can a godly heart manifest in speech creating peace, not strife. Throughout Chapter 4 James declares a God-centered heart pursues humility and service. The final section of Chapter 5 from verses 13 to 20 centers on the indispensable role of prayer. God speaks to us in nature, through mature believers, in the Bible, and during our times of meditation and prayer. A committed Christian walk cannot occur without consistent and constant prayer. We cannot fully turn to God or truly understand His will, unless we make an effort to have a vibrant prayer life. This beautiful book of James ends on the perfect theme to bring everything together.

Prayer is the essence of patience and perseverance. By its very nature prayer is submission to God—humility. When humbled before God you submit to God's timing, which requires patience. Prayer is also a power impacting the world and changing lives. Whether someone is suffering or happy, going to God in prayer and praise demonstrates a godly heart to the world (verse 13). If someone is ill, pray to God on their behalf because the faithful prayer of believers can uplift (verses 14–15).

Verse 15 deserves special attention because it can easily be misinterpreted: "And the prayer of faith will save the sick, and the Lord will raise him up. And if he has committed sins, he will be forgiven." In the first sentence of the verse, James is referring to spiritually restoring a fellow believer (Walvoord, 1983). The key context clue is the second clause of raising him up. This is not referring to actual physical restoration but rather spiritual uplifting. The first sentence also is not referring to salvation. I have stated it before but it bears repeating: the book of James is not discussing salvation but rather spiritual growth and its impact on our relationship with others (character and conduct), and this verse needs to be taken in this context. Further, this section of Chapter 5 is focused on our interaction with others. Obviously, then, within this context the second sentence of the verse also is not referring to salvation but rather the redress of grievances between believers. The second sentence is not saying prayer forgives sins, which it cannot because such a thing belongs to God and the forgiveness of sins was done once and for all by Christ's full propitiation on the cross at Calvary when He redeemed mankind and enabled the free gift of grace. This second sentence is saying relational restoration is possible through prayer. One of prayer's most powerful effects is to bring peace between people. If someone has wronged you, the quickest way to repair the relationship is to pray for them, which inherently includes forgiveness.

The importance of relationships cannot be overstated. Believers are not called to walk their spiritual journey as a lonely wanderer on a deserted road, but instead to join with other believers in meaningful fellowship. Talk and share with one another, confide and confess, and, of course, pray with and for one another (verse 16). It's important as a resource for uplifting and emotional healing to have a network of people on whom you can lean and in whom you can trust, which is precisely why James is so correct when he declares the importance of cultivating both character and conduct. If conduct does not match spiritual growth, our ability to be a valuable and trusted resource to other believers will be limited. Strong relationships are built on the solid rock of believers who cultivate growth in their character and conduct. Meaningful relationships are also built on prayer: "The effective, fervent prayer of a righteous man avails much." (verse 16) Prayer works because God answers them; of course He may answer no or He may say wait but God wants you to have conversations with Him and to draw closer to Him: "Be anxious for nothing, but in everything by prayer and supplication, with thanksgiving, let your requests be made known to God." (Philippians 4:6) God may indeed grant your exact desires (verses 17–18), but from personal experience I can testify He often will provide what is wanted but in an unexpected way not understood until later. I can also relay from experience and the Bible (Psalm 37:4) *effective* prayer means changing personal requests to God-centered ones.

James ends the book on one of the more important aspects of fellowship: when one falls short or strays from the righteous path (verses 19–20). God will move mountains to get believers to grow closer to Him, and a spiritual journey is never a straight path over smooth pavement but rather its unpaved trail goes over hills and into steep valleys. God knows this; He knows we are going to make mistakes and bad decisions. We are still forgiven, but God does expect lessons to be learned and attempts to be better in the future, to use trials and tough times to grow in our faith and develop perfect faith, which is exactly how James began his book. God uses many avenues to correct His children and to get them back on the righteous path: circumstances, the tugging of the Holy Spirt on the heart, and the advice of other believers are three very common ones. James highlights the last one: "If anyone among you wanders from the truth, and someone turns him back, let him know that he who turns a sinner from the error of his way will save a soul from death and cover a multitude of sins." (verses 19–20) It is incredibly important to support and uplift, to show compassion and empathy, which is why James devoted so much space in the book to developing a godly, humble, patient heart. Doing so not only reflects spiritual growth, but your spiritual light so shines forth as to light up the world and glorify God by helping someone else achieve a closer relationship with Him.

My sisters have often asked me how I faced Mom's death with such strength, which of course has opened up wonderful opportunities to give testimony and talk about the awesome beauty of a close relationship with the Lord. The power of living in perfect faith will not only create your extraordinary life but inspire those around you.

Five Questions for Exploration

- How much emphasis do you place on pursuing wealth and possessions?
- How is God working in your life to convict you of the need for more patience?
- What practical steps can you take to be more patient?
- What role does prayer play in your life? How important is it? What practical steps can you take to enhance your prayer life?
- How brightly does your light shine? How can it burn brighter?

SUMMARY

Merely professing faith isn't enough for a Christian walk to be fully committed. True devotion to the faith requires cultivation of the heart—right character— and proper interaction with the people around you— right conduct. Turning to God and seeking His will, especially during trials, converts a difficult time into an opportunity to develop perfect faith. Consciously expanding such perfect faith to all areas of life creates a truly humble, patient, God-filled heart. Your beautiful, godly heart must express itself in right conduct. Rather than show partiality, be courteous and compassionate to all. Allow God to tame your tongue and use words to uplift and help. Promote peace, not strife. Work to fulfill God's will and not your own selfish and greedy desires. Be patient. Pray consistently and constantly. A humble, patient, and godly heart is a life in service to others. When a believer develops right character and exudes right conduct, the light within glows like a thousand suns. Your life is filled with peace, joy, and contentment, and others experience the great glory of God. The world will be a better place for having you in it, which is the ultimate takeaway from the amazingly wonderful book of James.

BIBLIOGRAPHY

Stanley, Dr. Charles F. (2007). *The Life Principles Bible*. New King James Version. Nashville, TN: Thomas Nelson Publishing.

The Holy Spirit.

Walvoord, John F. and Zuck, Roy B. (Eds.). (1983). *The Bible Knowledge Commentary*. Colorado Springs, CO: Cook Communications Ministries.